Vox Populi

poems by

Virginia Konchan

Finishing Line Press
Georgetown, Kentucky

Vox Populi

Copyright © 2015 by Virginia Konchan
ISBN 978-1-62229-838-9 First Edition
All rights reserved under International and Pan-American Copyright Conventions.
No part of this book may be reproduced in any manner whatsoever without written permission from the publisher, except in the case of brief quotations embodied in critical articles and reviews.

ACKNOWLEDGMENTS

Grateful acknowledgement is made to the editors of *Diode, iO: a Journal of New American Poetry, La Fovea, Radar Poetry, Tupelo Quarterly, Verse,* and *Wave Composition*, who first published excerpts ("B," "D," "L," O," "M," "N," "Q," "R," "S," "T," "U," "V," "W," "X," and Y") from this chapbook.

Editor: Christen Kincaid

Cover Art: Christy Lee Rogers

Author Photo: Michael Dar

Cover Design: Elizabeth Maines

Printed in the USA on acid-free paper.
Order online: www.finishinglinepress.com
   also available on amazon.com

Author inquiries and mail orders:
Finishing Line Press
P. O. Box 1626
Georgetown, Kentucky 40324
U. S. A.

Table of Contents

A is for Amoeba 1
B is for Blamelessness 2
C is for Corporations 3
D is for Dynasty 4
E is for Elliptical 5
F is for Failure 6
G is for Gas-Lighting 7
H is for Hermaphrodites 8
I is for Iodine 9
J is for Jezebel 10
K is for Kraken 11
L is for Loretta Lynn 12
M is for Machiavell 13
N is for Narcocorridos 14
O is for Odysseus 15
P is for Pinafores 16
Q is for Quintessence 17
R is for Rationed Goods 18
S is for Somatic Pain 19
T is for Tristes Tropiques 20
U is for Ujjayi Pranayama 21
V is for Vox Populi 22
W is for Watergate 23
X is for Xanax 24
Y is for Yen 25
Z is for Zygotes 26

"Every dead letter still dreams of animation."
—*Susan Stewart*

A is for amoeba, auto-correct of the leitmotif, asset price bubbles, aristocracy and architecture: structural design, as distinct from expressionist rage. Aligning my printer page, I asked Allah, Buddha, Christ: make me more than a copyist of Archimedean proofs, my skin the sleek non-resisting elision of serial commas, accuracy of transmission as amanuensis my glorified secretarial goal. Honorary and dues-paying member of the actor's guild, I avow history's rerun, low-budget production of talking heads in airless parliamentary chambers of so-called state, monopolistic tyrants violating anti-trust statutes until forced to abdicate, as was King Lear, their nepotistic crowns.

B is for blamelessness, Sherlock's whodunit
hook keeping bee-hived housewives propped
up on one elbow past midnight, while their
husbands, laid-off from the plastic plant,
snore steadily on. B is for boring holes
into drywall in a modular, pre-fab home.
B is for the blasphemy of Cold War shelter—
as if a bomb could destroy language,
our belief in babies, biofuel, bric-brac,
and the helium balloon, now punctured,
of speculative financiers, cartoonish
voice-over whiting out, for decades,
the warp and woof of world.

C is for corporations assigned personhood, seeking
tax shelters, bail-outs, and banks in Luxembourg
and Andorra in which to deposit extorted feed.
C is for circumspect attorneys with careful
enunciation and smooth, sovereign smiles,
defending criminals before the prosecution,
witness, stenographer, and militia, watching
from an orbiting satellite or underground
submarine. C is for CNN and Foxconn:
rigged conglomerates, sating curiosity
on the subject, eternal, of greed.
The ruined republic's flummoxed
heat races to the spine's bottom
rung: then, sphinx-like, expels
toxic waste in its ascension to
the mind's pore (the eye).

D is for dynasty, enlightened despots in fluted collars
waving white kerchiefs from a balcony, sacrificial
ablutions performed by Alyosha Karamazov,
sainthood and its double, demonology,
inscribed in Dostoevskian tomes. D:
the drunken hour, Rumi at the wheel,
all catafalque and remonstrance (*"Out beyond ideas
of wrongdoing and rightdoing there is a field. I'll meet
you there"*), dawning of diurnal rounds,
dastardly elements in the periodic table
(*dubnium*) essential to life yet not naturally
occurring until death. D: the decision
we make to love the dustbowl that is
the stalled engine of the duct tear,
which, if active, would water,
with delphiniums, *mes devoirs:*
to etch the names, now effaced,
on the graves of Lord Regents
thrown from windows during
the defenestration of Prague.

E is for elliptical machines piled up in basements:
a lifetime spent running in place, not knowing
a war against one's body, once began, is an
unwinnable war. Step on, *homo economicus*:
the surface is black and slick, like eels, error,
and the screen of Grand Theft Auto,
paused at the elimination round.
E: electromagnetic induction,
static crackle after a lifetime of
chopping logs for the fire and
heating up of *eau-de-vie* for one's
weekly bath, on the stove. Welcome
to the 19th century, idea of value
no longer backed by solid gold but
use- and exchange value, currency
now circulating in subterranean
vaults of speculative markets
and computer hard drives:
filthy lucre passed from
screen to screen, and,
after market liquidation,
again from hand to hand.

F is for failure of fiduciary funds,
hullabaloo of the derivative market
drowned at sea, despite lifeboats,
by wave after susurrus wave.
F is for fencing, rhythm
of riposte, for fanfare
unchecked by economies
of need, desire, and time.
F is for *faiblesse*: the sin,
mortal, of Enron and
Monsanto executives,
sentenced to six months
in minimum security prison
for thieving pensioners.
Silent, the amphitheater
for cinema's dénouement,
unable to frame *fin-de-siècle*
warlords of investment
banking as villains,
(nor the investors,
as victims), anymore.

G is for gas-lighting, the spell under which
you convince me I'm crazy for liking to live,
sunny-side-up cognate between to speak
(gag binding mouth), while doubled-over
my own exteriorized consciousness (a lie).
G is for Garth Brooks, golems, and gastric
bypasses: the effort, inscribed in tomes
(e.g. Malebranche's *The Search After Truth*)
to say two or three words: *I exist, or will,*
the insistent pulse of declarative intent
marked credit in your black ledgermain,
where speech acts stands for X, and
done deeds, for Y. *Parole* matters,
but not nearly as much as *Langue,*
linguistic matter's matrix granting
clemency before the guillotine of
Abraham's inexorable hand
severed the head of the lamb.

H is for Hermaphrodites, factory-induced
haste, and helios, scorching the tongue.
H: the will to harm, bodies harangued by
Hussain for years, heteronormative man
hanging motionless on his hook like the
tender meat in a Francis Bacon frieze,
quivering, as if still animate or alive.
Hair on the arm standing up: marks
on the body (insignia or stigmata)
bearing down. You turn your head
from our battery-operated love:
zombies have always borne
the sight of Lazarus, stumbling
forth into sunlight, with unease.

I is for iodine, Crimean salt caves
from the Black Sea curing your
flagging will to live. I: the averring
angel above our bed, morning's
aubade inviolate despite a lifetime
spent in the invection oven, clay body
wrapped in mosquito netting, so as to
protect the prototypical self from view.
I: immunity, political asylum, *dasein*
no longer bound by Heideggarian
law, mea culpa ad infinitum and
free as only a portmanteau
carrying *Confederacy of
Dunces* (Ignatius Reilly's
irascible textual body,
transpositioned to
the parodic key
of C) can be.

J is for Jezebel, history's hallowed
whore pattering shyly down the
corridor of history in jellyfish
sandals, demanding three
square meals a day, and
the opportunity to labor
(skilled or un-), to survive.
J: jugular, what you sever
when my tenderer parts
are rendered inaccessible
by bluewitch nightshade,
Latin Solanum's deadly plant.
Cut the cord, unleash the crankshaft,
let the jukebox speakers swell, symphonically,
on the day when the ghost writer gives up
her unpaid rôle as democracy's amanuensis
(bonded labor), inserts her wages (a quarter)
into the slot, and, dancing over to the
Constitutional drafting table, replaces
Commonwealth with her proper name.

K is for Tennyson's Kraken:
cretin emerging, without fins,
from watery climes. Klimt's fame
sealed with his 1908 painting
The Kiss, housed in Vienna at the
Österreichische Galerie Belvedere.
K: the only letter to keep a straight
back while its two remaining limbs
squall, rooting for a truce between
hyla ("from the forest": paper, fuel)
and squid ink of Apollonic altitude.
The sun's dimmer switch, Jupiter,
kvetches: beta-god self-berating
as it keens toward oblivion (air).

L is for Loretta Lynn, red-haired crooner
singing *Coal Miner's Daughter* to a crowd
of one, her dead father, about growing up
on a hill in Butcher Holler with no one
to look after her but her beleaguered
mother, already worked to the bone.
Like a slingshot forged in hell,
until the past, present, and future
become a game rather than a prison,
barbed wire a technical effect, meant,
by the studio producer, to suggest
the difficulty of passage, the last aesthetic
sin that of showing seams, and, in life,
of obstructing a shopworn, tortured
body from leaving the factory floor
of the liminal, and finally
breaking through.

M is for Machiavelli, Marilyn Monroe,
the market price of meth, and icons
or monopolistic despots so notorious
as to enter lingua franca (the OED).
After Milton's paradisiacal trilogy
gave evil a personage and name,
rendering sedition a *fait accompli*,
he now defends the pious
against Lucifer's snares
(medieval torture in a
technocratic age), producing
matches in lieu of lamps,
and disposable goods in
lieu of nature, beauty, art:
sulfurous malodor from
a love of letters curing
the raw and rotten meat
of unrealized capital assets
(warehouses of 18mm film,
Western nude portraiture,
agricultural machines)
to trumpet the good news
of (eureka!) realized metaphor.

N is for narcocorridos: life's
sundry narwhals (heroin,
cocaine) as supplement to
the meat market's rib shanks:
industrialism's poisoned feed.
N is for nursing Rosemary's Baby,
humanimal recalling the shadow-self
of one's primogenitor, anti-matter at
cross-purposes with survival, pleasure,
and the will-to-need. Nipped in the bud,
the arc of *spiritus mundi:* nom de plume
of Niobe before trading in *nox aeterna*
for nirvana: markéd (lyric) time.

O is for Odysseus, whose name means trouble
in Greek, Phoenician language in the tradition
of diglossia, inscribed by the Cypriot syllabary
until the development, in the 9th century BC,
of the Greek alphabet. O: the opened
wound, tell-tale scar that betrayed
Odysseus on his ten-year journey
through the Ionian Islands and lairs
of Circe and Cyclops, *home* a foreign
tang on an oracular tongue craving
oysters, nicoise olives, and odd ends
from an open kitchen whose chef
prepares ox-tail soup for the return
of the wayfaring husband to the
once-ossified, now opening,
like ripened star anise, wife.

P is for pinafores, Pimm's cup cocktails
served with umbrellas pimping the rim.
P is for the patch-over, the pawnshop,
winding alleys leading to the dealer's
door, where he squats, grinning
and spitting snuff, knowing you've
returned for a pinch of oblivion,
Lethean potsherd: substances
making the mind gloat over
the recto verso body,
post-traumatic, stunned,
emitting pinpricks of light
in the eternal astral dark,
rotator cuff snapping
back into place, after
Hollywood's last biopic
(the Rapture), with
Copernican resolve.

Q is for quintessence, Quaaludes,
division of a census population
or mathematical quanta into fifths
for ease of sampling. Quixotic,
Quentin Tarnatino's camera,
glued to the cross-hatched iris
of Django, deadly pistoleer.
The epic quest: to rescue
his still-enslaved wife.
*Die Wahrheit wird
euch frei machen* . . .
Beneath the receipt of sale
for human life are legs,
broken stilts, a quill:
signatory deed of a
once-quiescent, now
quaking (*quelle horreur*)
polis, city, world.

R is for rationed goods, railcars, and the riptide of
the roaring twenties catching fire across New York,
Paris, Berlin, and London, in a respite of economic
prosperity before the Wall Street Crash of 1929:
Hoover gone stark raving mad,
Repressive State Apparatuses
flatlining a burgeoning America
(Jazz Age's strutting trombones,
sultry scat, Art Deco, disco,
foxtrot, well-lit allure of
rummy speakeasies
romanticizing ruin).
After Greenspan's introduction
of fiat currency—spin cycle
between austerity and stimulus,
equity and debt—relentless race
to the bottom rung of *redrum*,
Hollywood's red-eyed dawn.

S is for somatic pain, shellac of
armored bodies drying on
the battered *Santa Maria*
before the letters blur from
soot and rain. All aboard
the Pequod, hero's journey
reduced to satiric joust,
sodden mates of Ahab
shuddering, after battle,
on the silo's threshing floor.
Proletariat class rising
after being leveled by
labor inequity, on
the floor, unsutured
from the tilt-a-whirl
of the Mad Tea Party:
cartoon strip logic
of Walt Disney's
simulated world.

T is for Tristes Tropiques, travelogue of
Claude Levi-Strauss, world view of
anthropos teetering before falling
off the bias-cut of his totalizing tongue.
T: Tahiti's yawning orange sunsets
atop the 118 islands of French Polynesia,
once a site of colonial carnage (over half
the population decimated by disease in 1767):
now where vacationers go to be reborn.
T is for Tarantella (hooped skirts aflame),
termites, tornados and teamwork,
because alone life is impossible.
Together, more so, unless
tethered to the astronomical
clock created by Norweigian
Rasmus Sørnes: abstraction's
tipping point, the Trojan Horse
of the apocalypse, racing against
the *durée*, now exploded, of time.

U is for Ujjayi Pranayama
The magician's ruse is understood:
it is ujjayi pranayama, victorious
breath, that syncs each letter in
the Latin alphabet, yesterday
to today, and each stacked
vertebra on the column,
Grecian, of your spine.
U is for the turnstile
whereupon you realize
you have been traveling
with the wrong tribe
for 10,000 years,
lost in the Upanishads,
Orpheus' scattered body
a sacrificial corpus before
history's banned ur-text,
The Idiot's Guide to Usury,
ignited, not as if, but on, fire.

V: signal flare of Vox populi
again shining voluminous red,
wax figure's walkie talkie
veering out of range before
returning to the big-pharma
military industrial complex's
sealed compound: a people's
vernacular, in quarantine.
V is for vespers, vigilance
perpetual, of *Le Bonheur*,
Virgil's vertiginous volta
guiding sheep through
the vernal equinox's
Venn diagram. V:
amped-up Victrola
the soundtrack to
performative pomp,
vigorous outpouring
of Mercutio, Caesar,
and Richard III's
(vampires, all)
crocodile tears.

W is for Watergate, twisted arm of
realpolitik finally breaking with the
media's police state, warbling voice
of penitent politicos an emergency
siren stuck on pitch of panic. Clamor
of complaint, meet euphony's restraint,
what appears beneath the waitress garb:
the body's webbing, svelte ligaments
of proto-industrial design. *Why* is not
a question we ask, whittling whalebone
for the corset of Wittgenstein's bride,
not as equation or game, but to avert
world systems collapse. Filmic trace
of Wall Street cons seen in 1988's
A Fish Called Wanda, heist-comedy
set in London. "America is not always
a winner," prophesied Archie,
diamond robber extraordinaire,
"Just look at the Vietnam War."

X is for Xanax, xenophobes,
and x-rays that purport
to shine a cathode light
on the pathologies
of your spine. X:
positus, topoi, key—
secret location of the eye-
witness to the century's
most gruesome crime.
Let those for whom
gender and speech
are propositional acts
sing of the headless,
stateless, nameless,
exiled in St. Tropez
until discovered by
satellite topography:
phosphorescent
eyeball of fame,
tungsten blue on
the screen of our
illicit, private-cum-
public desires.

Y is for yen, Japan's reserve
currency alongside the U.S.
dollar, euro and pound sterling.
Made out of 100% aluminum,
the 1 yen coin can float on water.
Y is for Yosemite's brash yellows,
universal symbol of sun praised
by drought survivors, demi-gods,
and ancient sequoia trees.
Y: the yearning for solvency,
freedom from deadly ghosts
(simulacrum, creditism),
yesteryear's capital flows
confronting the Yukon
River's banks, tourniquet
of *terra firma* saving the
human species, six feet under,
from the quicksand of Keynesian
(market-managed) history.

Z is for zygote, atoms
shuttling from meiosis to
mitosis at the speed of
light, in an archegonia
or Porphyria tree. The
human bestiary: a long-waged,
oedipal war, decisive victory
given to the committee-approved
prodigal, ousting the lemmings
shuttling between one and zero
in a binary programmatic code.
La Gloire: Zelda Fitzgerald, after
reading the Great American novel
(blinking price signal of a bankrupt
state siphoning surplus from slaves),
up and fled, *roman à clef* an homage
to history from beginning to end:
Murder She Wrote, she wrote;
Thus Spake Zarathustra, she said.

Virginia Konchan's poems have appeared in *The New Yorker*, *Best New Poets*, *The Believer*, *Boston Review*, *The New Republic*, *Verse*, and elsewhere. She lives in Montreal.